SAMUEL
AND THE **LITTLE PEOPLE**

By Arnold James Isbister

ESCHIA BOOKS

© 2021 by Eschia Books Inc. & Arnold Isbister

All rights reserved. No part of this work covered by the copyrights hereon may be reproduced or used in any form or by any means—graphic, electronic or mechanical—without the prior written permission of the publisher, except for reviewers, who may quote brief passages. Any request for photocopying, recording, taping or storage on information retrieval systems of any part of this work shall be directed in writing to the publisher.

The Publisher: Eschia Books Inc.
Library and Archives Canada Cataloguing in Publication
Title: Samuel and the little people / by Arnold James Isbister.
Names: Isbister, Arnold J., author.
Identifiers: Canadiana (print) 2021037229X | Canadiana (ebook) 20210374942 | ISBN 9781990321092 (softcover) | ISBN 9781990321108 (PDF)
Subjects: LCSH: Dwarfs (Folklore)—Canada—Juvenile literature. | LCSH: Fairies—Canada— Juvenile literature. | LCSH: Folklore—Canada. | CSH: First Nations—Canada—Folklore.
Classification: LCC E98.F6 I83 2021 | DDC j398.2089/97—dc23

Project Director: Dianne Meili
Cover Image: Arnold James Isbister
Image Credits: Arnold James Isbister
Layout Design: Ryschell Dragunov
Cover Design: Greg Brown

Produced with the assistance of the Government of Alberta.

We acknowledge the financial support of the Government of Canada.
Nous reconnaissons l'appui financier du gouvernement du Canada.

PC: 38-1
Printed in China

Contents

Foreword, by Maria Campbell . . 6

The Journals of Samuel
White Wolf 13

1. We Were Giants 17
2. Mrs. J Talks 33
3. Fire and Deep Water 43
4. Napaysis, A Communion . . . 57
5. A Time to Ask 67
6. Lost in the City 75
7. The Old Storyteller 103

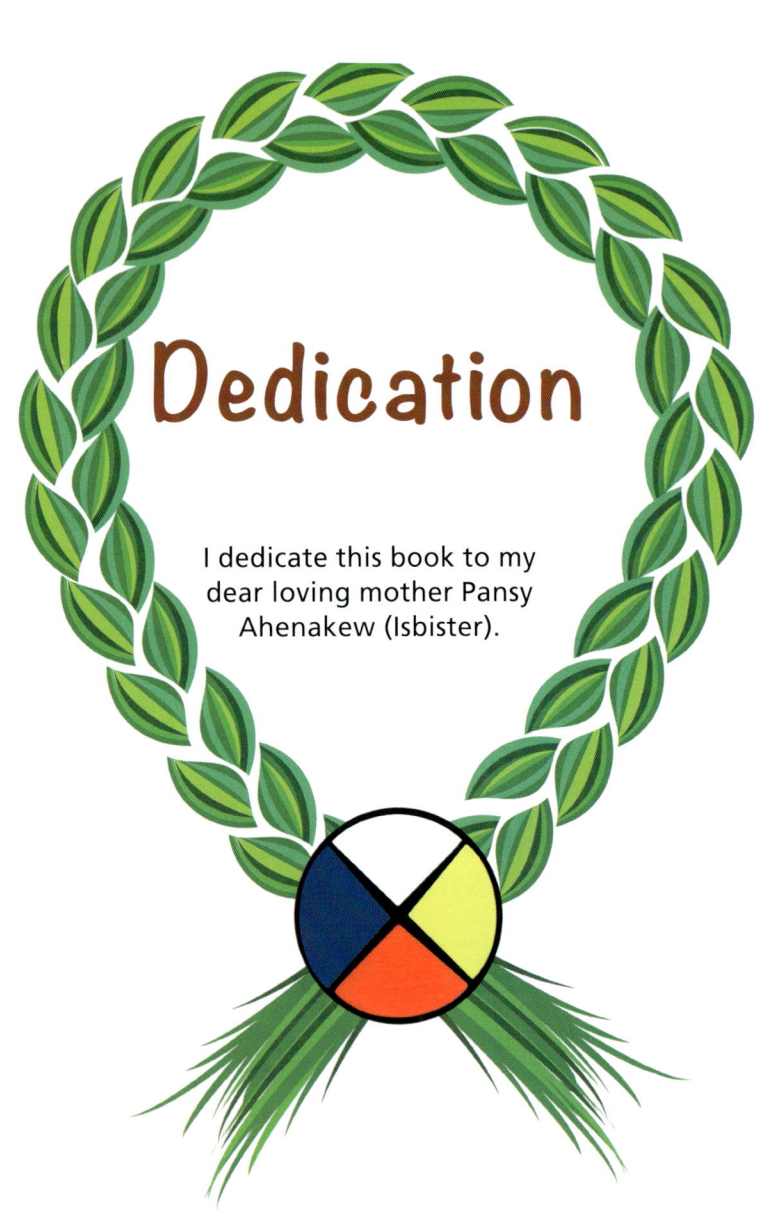

Dedication

I dedicate this book to my dear loving mother Pansy Ahenakew (Isbister).

Acknowledgements

This book was accomplished by the hard work of Dianne Meili of Eschia Books, who encouraged my writing on the Little People. I must acknowledge too, our Elders and all Moshums and Kokums across this great land for keeping our culture and history through your stories. This book is just a fraction, a stone, in the foundation of our identity. And a final thank you to Maria Campbell for her support.

Foreword

"Ay ni nay stoosin nichee. A kipi ke yoka chik mah mahkway see suk kesape. Puko kah nip ah se...

"Ninêstosin nicheechee. Ê-kî pê kiyohkowicik mêmêkwayisîsak kîkisîpâyâk. Poko ka nipâsiyân. I am so tired my Cheechee. The Little People came to visit me this morning. I just have to sleep for awhile."

My Cheechum murmured a few more words and sank down into her sleeping mat. She pulled the blanket over her tiny frame and promptly fell into a deep sleep.

"Cheechum wihtamowin kîkway ispayik, kâya nipa!" I shook her. "Cheechum tell me what happened. Don't sleep!"

But she was out, and from eight years of being her granddaughter, I knew there was no waking her up. My Cheechum slept as hard as a winter bear when she napped and especially if she had been visiting—not just any old visitors—but the Little People. I raced out to tell all my siblings and cousins.

There are many nations of Little People, across our land—and like us who are Cree, Métis, Dene, Assinaboine and Saulteaux—they each had their own names with language and cultural differences. But, according to our Cheechum, they could also communicate with humans

because they had stayed true to their old ways. Some of them were kind and gentle while others could be mean and suspicious of everything and everybody. Others were shy and most often were never seen. Cheechum's visitors were called mêmêkwayisîsak. They were smaller than most, curious; friendly if they liked you; and had a great love of human things such as needles, thread, beads, tea and especially sugar and raisins.

On this visit, she had given them all the raisins mom was saving and told us about her gift to them.

"Kamiyo ispayihkonaw êkwa. We will have good luck now."

Dad had laughed and said they better bring us good luck because Cheechum's gift of all the raisins meant no pie for her birthday—which is what mom was saving them for.

That evening as the old people sat around drinking their last cup of tea, they told stories of the different encounters they had, or had heard about the little people. Some of them lived by the rivers they said—their homes deep in the small caves and tunnels on the steep banks. They were river travelers, paddling their tiny crafts into the currents and floating to their destinations. They were seldom seen on land, but the old people said they could be seen in the water in the very early mornings or late in the evenings. They were beautiful singers, one old lady said, and would sometimes be heard, their tiny, sweet voices drifting over the land.

"Mitoni takahkihtâkosiwak kikiskêyihtiyin ê-sawêyimikowisin kâ pihtawacik. They sound so beautiful—you just know you have been blessed when you hear them."

Others, called pikosîsak, were taller and lived in the forest close to the muskeg, the pine trees and the tamarack. They loved the pitch from those trees and used it for most everything, including medicine. That was where our old uncle Patrice got the medicine he used on his horses and for people. Nearly everybody, from the oldest to the youngest, had stories of how they had been doctored with just boiled piko. Piko means the pitch or sap that hangs in strings or in little bunches on the trees. It also made a wonderful chewing gum when uncle mixed it with vanilla. It cleaned your teeth, making them gleam as white as snow. But you had to have the recipe—the pikosîsak had given Uncle Patrice the recipe in exchange for snuff. Dad said piko was also used in olden times to seal the seams when making canoes.

And then there was Cheechum's mêmêkwayisîsak. We never saw them, but we loved them because she loved them. Whenever we were on the land, especially by the lakes, we would always leave beads or long lengths of mom's embroidery thread. We always had these in our pockets for offerings so they would take care of us as we went about setting our rabbit snares or picking berries and pakânak (wild nuts).

There were others, too, but our people only knew the local ones who lived among us. I never saw one in my entire life until many years later when

I became a grandmother. My first grandchild, Thomas John Edward Oliver—TJ for short—and his two friends Steven and Luke came across an old, old man sitting on a big rock in the middle of the south Saskatchewan River when they were about eight years old. They had been playing just upstream from Gabriel´s Crossing when they came running home to tell us. They said the old man looked at them, and when they asked him if he was fishing, dove into the water and never came up. They were scared he had drowned because he was so old.

While my friend Beth Cuthand—the boys' mom—called the RCMP, I raced out with the boys to the place where the old man had jumped into the water. When Beth arrived with the RCMP they looked everywhere but saw nothing. And when the boys described the old man as being about a foot tall with long, long hair and a beard, the police laughed.

"Sounds like some old elf," one of them said to the other, and they left.

That evening an elder from One Arrow Reserve dropped by for a visit. We told him about the old man, and he wasn't the least bit surprised. He told us that this was one of the places where the mêmêkwayisîsak had been seen over the years. He said when he was a boy, the old people had many stories about them, but like everywhere else, these stories were seldom told anymore. He told the boys they were very fortunate because not many people ever saw them, even in olden times.

Several years later, my brother Wil and I went with an old man from Chitek Lake to another location on the river, where he did a ceremony for the little people. He said he had just finished a Sun Dance where he had been instructed to come to where I lived and ask me to take him to the place where the mêmêkwayisîsak lived.
I had been shown the place earlier in my life by another old man, but I had only been there once to leave offerings of thread, thimbles and food. As the old man talked, I knew I had been shown that place just for him, and so, I took him there.

I will always remember that day. The bright sunshine and loud chirping of the birds as we arrived at the location and how, as my brother and I sat down on the ground, and the old man opened his bundle and began preparing his pipe, the chirping and singing stopped. The silence was incredible. You know how sometimes you can hear silence?

When it was over and we got up to leave, the birds started chirping and singing again. I will never forget the overwhelming humility and gentleness I felt as we walked back to the car. The old man left, and I never saw him again. Today there is a building backed up against the hill blocking the doorway where the mêmêkwayisîsak lived.

It is important to find and take care of wild places still left on the land; there are not many left. It is our responsibility to keep the land and water clean. Hold it up, protect it and protect all the wahkomâkanak—the relatives you see and do

not always see. Leave little offerings in special places for them. You will know them when you come across them. Don't ask if the feeling is real; just believe it. Little people are Protectors of the Earth, and they carry many earth teachings. Just listen to them.

Enjoy Arnold's stories. They are miyo âcimowinamiyo, good stories; and miyo maskihhkiy, good medicine.

Êkosi pitamâ, enough for now

Maria Campbell
October 10, 2021
Gabriel's Crossing

I came across Samuel White Wolf in my research of Up-See-So Ai-See-Neh-Suk, the word for Little

The Journals of Samuel White Wolf

(1856–1950)

Samuel and the Little People

People in my Cree language. Throughout my childhood, I had a few experiences with the Little People, and I needed to know more about them. Their existence is a myth—a legend—to many Indigenous people across North America, and in fact, similar stories about them are found worldwide. The Little People are a peace-loving species with a supernatural ability to communicate with animals and fortunate humans to whom they give comfort, companionship and predictions of the future. I have heard reports of them misleading people or influencing them to perform misdeeds, but those I met were kind and helpful.

Descriptions of Up-see-So Ai-See-Neh-Suk are vague and assorted. I think this is natural since they are usually seen by individuals who describe them according to their own perception. Sightings by groups are rare. Many have seen their tiny footprints—perhaps around abandoned home sites—but few, especially in our civilized society, have had individual encounters.

Mr. White Wolf, as it turns out, is an ancestor of mine. I discovered his journal in my deceased moshum's (grandfather's) belongings kept by our family. His name was often mentioned in family history conversations, but I never heard of him having a connection to the Little People. I am sure there were stories, but over time, generations took less and less interest in them, considering them tales of delusion and nonsense.

I have had experiences with the Little People, so I decided to bring Samuel's journal to light, transcribing them from Cree syllabics into English.

The Journals of Samuel White Wolf

I hope his life experiences enrich your life and help you to believe there is more—much more—to our (sometimes) mundane lives than we think here in the physical realm.

—Arnold James Isbister

We Were Giants

CHAPTER 1

We Were Giants

"Napaysis?" I asked cautiously.

"Call me Nap. We're good friends now. It's quicker to say."

"Okay…Nap?"

"Hey, don't say it too much," he joked, his laughter sounding tiny and bright. "You'll wear it out." He punched my leg with his child-sized fist, and I barely felt it.

"Where do you come from? How did you come to be, and why are you still here? People say Up-See-So Ai-See-Neh-Suk are fiction, myth, only real in ancient legends that died many, many generations ago?"

We Were Giants

I studied him as we walked, realizing I had come to care deeply about this little blue-skinned, no-necked person who protected me and kept me entertained.

Napaysis thought a bit then stopped. "Let me tell you a story, Sam. You can write it if you wish."

I did wish, so we sat on the grass, and I pulled out my tattered diary to capture his words.

"Into the far reaches of time, things were magical, you know. Not like today..."

I interrupted Napaysis. "Some of my Elders are still pretty magical. They can make it rain if they want. My moosum can call forth a strawberry plant to grow in the snow if he needs the runners to make a medicine."

"Of course. But I am talking about a time when animals talked to humans. When the forests of trees were magical places, and anything could happen. When everyone believed."

I nodded and felt sheepish for interrupting my friend. He smiled at me and continued.

In a magical forest, there lived a beautiful girl of a medicine tribe, known for their magical abilities. Her name was "Walks Far." She was appointed by her Elders to go forth and see the world and bring back any news to benefit them or to note things, or beings to avoid.

Samuel and the Little People

Like her kind, she grew to be petite, tiny with dark hair and eyes. She was of the Little People, or Up-See-So Ai-See-Neh-Suk, but ages before they were known as the Enchanted Ones for their goodness and generosity, and…they were once giants. They had everything needed to live and were endowed with supernatural powers when all was created. They used their power to help others, as was intended, but it came with a cost. Every time they used magic, the people as a whole would shrink in size, and their powers diminished bit by bit. With each act of "medicine power" they changed slightly, from a healthy, bronzed tan to blue and green, and shrinking in size. Their eyes grew larger over thousands of years to what you see today.

From the days of our ancestors, the tribes talk of them as being giants who walked with the mystic trees. Now they ride on the backs of wild cats and coyotes, skittering into the branches and leaves of those same trees to hide. It was their fate to disappear, vanish forever, unless they found a way to save themselves. By necessity they became unseen, hidden in the moss and foliage so as not to encounter those vain people who asked them for selfish favours—which they are bound by the Creator to honour—thus using up their life force needlessly. Such was their isolated and invisible existence; other tribes began speaking of them as a myth from the past. The Up-See-So Ai-See-Neh-Suk Elders knew their future was uncertain and that they must somehow marry into other clans and tribes to survive. With the difference in size, marriage among clans and tribes seemed impossible, and the Elders began to lose hope.

We Were Giants

Marriage to other groups should have happened long ago, but fear and ignorance of their gifts prevented this. Already they had diminished in size so as to be powerless. Generations came, then were gone, and the Up-See-So Ai-See-Neh-Suk became so small that they did not venture from the forest. Yet, a shred of magic still existed among the trees and plants.

Napaysis stopped and looked around him.

So, one day, born of urgency, the Elders sat down under a grove of trees and put out a call for all to gather. And gather they did. In the thousands! They sat in the trees, and you could hear the rustling of leaves as they moved among the branches that bowed to the earth with their weight. These trees became known as Weeping Birch and are still around today.

Napaysis turned, smiled at me and indicated I should write down this bit of knowledge.

From the north, a great white owl glided to the ground with Walks Far on its back. Then the meeting started. Many ideas and plans were shared, but it wasn't until dawn that they agreed upon a solution. With what magic they still possessed, they put their hopes in Walks Far, giving her a full-sized human

Samuel and the Little People

body and looks so that she could enter into the outer world unquestioned. The Ancient Ones warned her that the change was not permanent and would fade in the coming months. "Your time amongst the humans is limited," they told her. "And so, we are sending our winged friends—the owls, loons, crows and ravens—to fly great distances and find you a suitable man of genteel values so as to shorten the time you will be enchanted."

Napaysis paused, then added, "These winged ones can, and still do, carry messages from beyond our time and place." He ended, looking at me as if I had best remember this.

He continued.

In the Great Plains not too far away lived a young War Chief, a headman respected by many tribes. His name in Cree translated to mean Many Feathers because he had earned many Eagle feathers in wars and skirmishes with enemy bands. He was strong, tall and generous, but he had no wife. It was not that he didn't long for one, it was that none of the many

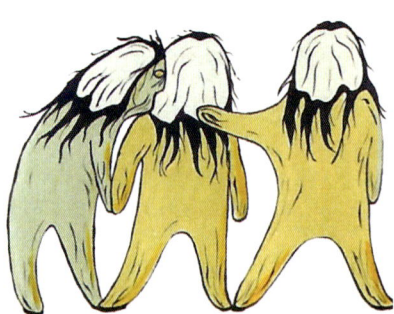

young girls brought to him by their fathers had managed to stir his heart. Deep inside, he knew there existed a partner who could fill his days with love and laughter and give him an heir. But so far, she had eluded him.

We Were Giants

As a long line of women came and went, he worried he would have to marry a woman he did not love. His father, the Grand Chief, was getting old, and the tribes united under him were restless, demanding the young War Chief select a woman from amongst their people to become their future Chieftess. Soon they became aggressive in competing for the honour of having one of their own selected; war or revolution was looming unless their War Chief married.

In urgency, after much thought, he visited his mother who was wise in affairs of the heart. She listened, then searched in her parfleche bags for an old, beaded leather case, retrieving from it a small black stone she then held in her outstretched palm. She told him it was a gift from the Little People, and she used to wish upon it when she was a girl. She handed it to him, telling him to place it under his pillow at night and sleep on it. "The answer may come to you in a dream," she told him.

He did as she directed and dreamed about a majestic owl and an enormous birch tree that shone and whispered as its leaves shook. Under its giant arms, he saw little people, small as foxes, and among them a woman radiant in her beauty. She glided to and fro in the rays of sunshine, darting quickly, and was as daring as a hummingbird. His eyes fixed on her, taking in her obsidian hair and her wise and kind amber eyes that saw into his soul. Into his dream he fell, and he fell in love with the way she carried herself in magnificent splendour. Around her arms were braided bands of reed, rings of wood woven to hold coloured stones, the likes of which he had never seen. Her slim figure was clothed

Samuel and the Little People

in a lustrous gown sewn with tiny stitches from the single hide of an elk and glowing white in his vision. He knew she was exceptional, special to her tribe. With that thought, he awoke.

Many Feathers exclaimed, "That's her! She is the young woman I am to marry!"

He knew with certainty that she was the one, but where was he to search? He stopped hunting and warring, instead spending his time travelling and scouring the plains and valleys in search of her. He did so in vain. Dismayed, and after months of sleeping in the rain and living on what small game he could carry, he rode into unfamiliar lands. One night, while lighting his evening fire to cook a skinny rabbit he had managed to snare, he looked up to see a great white owl fly above him and perch on the limb of a tree. Recalling his dream, he followed the owl as it flew away and landed some distance away in the branches of a giant birch towering in a meadow. Approaching, he saw a slight figure sitting under the tree. Her beauty stunned him; he had found her.

Dismounting, he knelt before Walks Far. "I have searched far and wide since you came to me in my dream. I am a War Chief of the united tribes. My name is Many Feathers."

With a slight bow, she reached for his hand. "I am called Walks Far of the Little People."

"I have heard of your people, but I thought the story was a myth." He pondered her size. In his dream she was tiny, but here she rose from the

We Were Giants

ground to stand tall and beautiful. And why was she alone?

"We are of the forest, seldom seen," Walks Far answered.

Many Feathers was certain this was the girl from his dream and knew he must act on this blessed meeting without seeming too eager. "Please be my guest at our camp so that we may get to know each other. Your safety and chastity will be guarded by my honour." He bowed graciously and backed away, waiting for her reply.

"I feel we are fated to meet. So yes, I accept your invitation."

He offered his horse for her comfort, and the two journeyed to his territory, her trusted great white owl flying after them. Arriving amongst his people, he introduced her to his mother and father and then the rest of his tribe. All grew fond of this graceful guest and could not help but notice she would be the perfect wife for Many Feathers. They noted how her love for him shone in her eyes, and they gave Many Feathers their blessing.

Soon, as he marvelled at his great luck in finally finding the woman he had dreamed of, he asked her to be his wife. She loved him but was acutely aware of the enchantment placed upon her by her people. She knew there must be no lies or secrets between her and Many Feathers. She told him she must think about the proposal and ask her Elders for their blessing. Fearful that she might not come back to him if she returned to her people, he insisted on

Samuel and the Little People

escorting her. She remained steadfast that she must go alone, and all was prepared for her travel the next day. The War Chief, dismayed at her decision, could not sleep. After smoking his small pipe, he ventured out in the early light of the morning to dissuade her from leaving.

But he was too late. She was gone! Devastated and broken, he fell to the ground. By dawn, he had regained his composure and ordered his dog soldiers to find her. Days of searching were futile. When he first found her in the magic meadow, she had not told him where her home was, and now he might never know. For three days, he waited, not sleeping. The thought of her not returning was becoming real, and he languished in sorrow. Thoughts of death entertained him while he wallowed in his darkness; to live without her was inconceivable. Mired in his dark thoughts, he was almost deaf to a soft familiar voice that floated to him on a breeze.

It was her! Turning every which way, he could see no one; he listened with his whole heart to the whisper in the dark.

"I love you, Many Feathers," Walks Far said. Then, becoming more composed, she stepped out of the dark shadows. "I must tell you something."

The young chief sensed her distress, interjecting with his own pledge. "I love you, too! I thought I had lost you forever. Please, never leave me again." He spoke more passionately than he ever had in his life.

We Were Giants

"Let me speak." Her tone was crystal clear as she took his hand. "I travelled home to talk with my People, to let them know I had found my love. And they were happy, overjoyed, to hear my good fortune. My People are the ancient Giants who became the Little People, the Up-See-So Ai-See-Neh-Suk, of your tales. We have magic, but the magic is dying slowly as we use it. Once we were giants but grew smaller as we used the magic; it became our curse. Now we must use it to survive, and that is why you see me as your kind. I am enchanted to your size now, but I am small in my world. In time, we will all disappear."

"It does not matter who or what you are. I love you!" the War Chief vowed. His eyes wet with tears, he promised to protect and stay with her as his wife forever.

"That cannot be," she told him.

"Stay, please stay! Don't leave me…I will do anything to have you as my wife." He was kneeling now as a beggar.

"Anything?"

"Anything! Yes, anything!" Suddenly, he rose to his feet, the sparkle back in his eyes.

"There is one condition. There is also the truth to be told."

"What truth?"

"I will tell you, and then you must make your choice."

Samuel and the Little People

The Chief nodded, not wanting his newfound hope to vanish.

"The truth is my People arranged our first encounter so that we would meet. It is not coincidence. With magic, we entered your dream, where I introduced myself and laid a seed of charm; then the great white owl led you to me. What was not planned was that I would come to love you… and love you greatly. That is why I must tell you everything."

The Princess bowed her head, pausing to hear Many Feathers speak his truth.

"Before you continue, you must know that I love you, too, and it comes not from some charm or magic but from the heart! My heart and mind are true and honest. Your seed planted was but a vision to enlighten me…to show the way."

His eyes pleaded with hers as she spoke again.

"And…there is one condition, something that is set in stone. It is not of my doing or of my People's wishes, but it is what we are left with. We have little magic remaining, so this is all we can do." Walks Far paused to let the gravity of what she was about to say sink in. The War Chief listened in earnest.

"I am as your kind now, but as the magic fades, I will return to my People. I will marry you, Many Feathers and mother your child, but I can stay for only two years, after which the magic spell dies. Can you marry me knowing this?"

We Were Giants

"Yes!" he exclaimed, hearing her words yet not comprehending how he would feel when the spell ended.

"You must understand, my love. There is no other way."

"Yes, I know. I understand!" Not willing to stop and consider the implications of her truthful message, he held her and would not let her go. He whispered his vow, "I will love you forever, no matter what."

So, they married, and all the territorial tribes attended the wedding; it was a historic event. Shortly thereafter, the young woman became pregnant and bore her husband a son, who was of full size. Both Up-See-So Ai-See-Neh-Suk and humans rejoiced. The boy was blessed with gifts from both worlds, and he would pass them on to many of his own children. A passion filled the land; all revelled in this good fortune. The War Chief indulged his blessed son with every toy to be found; the young mother nursed him, taught him and sang mystical lullabies to him that she composed. Friends professed to see a tiny glowing Spirit—a bright, dancing orb—when she sang. Above the mother and child, a great white owl landed and perched on a tree, and a loon harmonized with her voice from far away.

During that two years, all was beautiful until the fateful morning when she disappeared. Many Feathers, his heart breaking, searched for endless days and nights until he finally understood the true

Samuel and the Little People

meaning of her warning on the night he had asked her to marry him.

"I can stay for two years only," she had said.

It finally dawned on him that she meant it, and now she was gone forever. In her absence, her son grew to be a fine leader, stepping into the role of Grand Chief over all of the united tribes. With his son acting as the new leader, Many Feathers continued searching harder than ever for his missing wife. He disappeared for weeks at a time on his horse until one day he failed to return. Some would say they saw him in a distant land, following a great white owl.

Giants were nevermore. The Up-See-So Ai-See-Neh-Suk vanished, and magic died the day Walks Far left her husband. But if you listen, you can hear her songs carried on a gentle breeze that will enchant you, beguile your senses…and you will see.

Napaysis looked down.

That is how we survived, by sharing our gifts, our blood through her son and others. Mercifully, we stopped declining in size and powers, although we remain of the stature we are now—small and shrivelled, wrinkled and with pale blue-green skin from hiding in the tunnels, caves and bushes. Through thousands of years, we have become self-sufficient. We don't need anyone from the outside world. We have become timeless, that is to say our

We Were Giants

time is different from yours. But we get lonely, too, and we will socialize with certain people whom we choose to be with, and we will help those in need upon occasion.

At the end of Napaysis' story, I was perplexed. "But Nap, your people gave blood through marriage to others. You didn't receive any."

Napaysis smiled, "Oh, but we did. You forget. Where do you think the chief disappeared to? And there were two that were born: the full-sized boy and the tiny glowing one that friends saw when Walks Far sang. This little spirit was taken by the great white owl to her mother, Walks Far, to our home."

Napaysis turned his slender, wrinkled hands palm up, gazing deeply into my eyes as only he could.

"And we're still here," he whispered.

Mrs. J Talks

CHAPTER 2

Mrs. J Talks

The first stories I heard were disturbing. My friends, always trying to scare me, told me the Little People were vicious, ugly and would take children who were never seen again. But I had listened to adults telling stories of the same Little People, and they didn't come close to describing them as the monsters made up in kids' imaginations. So, although I was cautious, I was not terrified of coming upon one or two on my solitary walks in the forest or out with my father hunting or trapping.

In fact, I recall one summer day when we hitched up our horses and bumped along an old, rutted road in our creaking wagon to visit old Mrs. J. She lived at the far end of the lake where the cold depths were blamed for the disappearance of many men and

Mrs. J Talks

children. Tales about the dark waters where Mrs. J lived made me shiver, but I still wanted to travel past it and see it with my own eyes. No children were allowed there.

Mrs. J's last name was a long, tricky word to say in Cree, so we shortened it to Mrs. J. Mom and Dad often went to see her in the spring, summer and fall when she lived at her original home, alone at the far end of the lake. In the winter, she stayed with her daughter at a settlement close to us. My Dad cut wood for her stove, and chopped pine branches to dry the meat he brought her, providing she kept some venison for us. My mom gathered vegetable and flower seeds for Mrs. J to plant and gave her leftover jams from the winter before.

While we visited, Mrs. J baked bannock and cooked hamburger soup for us—the best soup I ever had. After our soup, we put the remaining bannock into the hot oven and then took it out to slather it with Mom's jam, such a treat with muskeg tea. Mrs. J was a great lady, so loving and caring, considering the many heartbreaks she'd endured. Years earlier, her son and husband John had perished in a howling blizzard. Priests had sent word their son was sick, so John hurried to bring him home, but the boy died before he arrived. Grieving, though the priests warned him against travelling in the storm blowing in, he left to return home, pulling his son's body behind his horse on a travois. John, becoming disoriented in the whipping wind and heavy snowfall, froze protecting his son's body. When the winds blew, the memories they stirred up in Mrs. J would send her travelling to our home at any hour of

Samuel and the Little People

the day or night. She was an Elder in age, but never seemed to get old as I recollect.

We arrived at Mrs. J's cabin before noon. Dad set about his chores, while Mom and I went inside to say hello. After a hug and some pleasantries, we sat down on some old chairs, the paint chipping away in flakes. The table was just some grey boards nailed together on top of four rickety legs, and it swayed when you put any weight on it.

"I knew you were coming today," Mrs. J said to my mother.

Mrs. J Talks

"Oh, did someone tell you?" my mom asked, looking around the tiny room.

"Ah huh," she answered. "The little ones…they told me you folks were coming today."

My mother studied her. She had heard stories of the Little People, but this was the first time she had spoken to someone who had just interacted with them.

"Up-See-So Ai-See-Neh-suk?" mother asked directly.

"Yes, those ones."

Mrs. J got busy setting the table and dishing out the food for our meal, but then she stopped and looked directly at me.

"You know who I mean, don't you Samuel?"

I nod as if what she and my mother were just talking about was completely normal. Right then I was more interested in what I spied across the dark room—a slab of bannock freshly baked and leaning at an angle against the stovepipe. I could also see through the dim light an old, red lard pail full of tea. Mrs. J slowly poured me some tea, broke off some bannock—still hot—and handed me the homemade butter and jam. Mmmm…it was so good!

While we nibbled our bannock and sipped muskeg tea, the adults used the time to catch up on what was going on "out there," who was doing what, who married, who died, where was "so-and-so" and whatever other news they might have to share.

Samuel and the Little People

Mrs. J was having a hard time with her knees and back, so she told me what she wanted done; her old finger bent with arthritis pointed to areas that needed my attention. I went to a small back room used for storage that hadn't been cleaned for a long time and began to arrange and stack things. Kneeling on a floor of rough boards, I looked up to see Mrs. J silhouetted in the weak light coming in through the cracked and dirty window, the room's only source of light. The film of smoke on the glass bathed everything in a dull blue colour, and I could see specks of dust floating in the ghostly sunlight.

Kneeling there, I could see her through the doorway motioning and talking in a whisper to someone I couldn't see. My eyes tried to pierce the darkness and the glare from the sun that blotted her out. I continued my chores, but I was curious about what Mrs. J was doing, so I edged myself closer to the door. I could see my mother in the kitchen facing away to the wall and Mrs. J crouched over, staring behind the stove at a wood pile left there for convenience. She appeared to be listening to something or someone, then nodded her head. Suddenly, she straightened up and slipped into her bedroom. This really piqued my curiosity so, without thinking, I stood up to follow her. She saw me and motioned for me to come in. I shuffled over to where she sat on her bed, patting a place beside her.

Reluctantly I sat down beside her, not sure what was happening.

"Did you see them, Samuel?" she asked.

I shook my head. "Who?"

Mrs. J Talks

"Those Little People," she said, turning her head to me as her eyes lingered on the dark corners of the room. "I saw you watching me, and you are maybe thinking I'm crazy?" She tapped her forehead with a bent finger. "But I'm not Sam. Let me tell you something."

Mrs. J put her hands on her lap, smoothing wrinkles from her apron.

"I call them Up-See-So Ai-See-neh-Suk—those people who are little."

Speaking in Cree, she explained they have been around for countless generations and are always talked about in whispers.

"My parents and their grandparents knew about them, but few talked for fear of being seen as "not right" or crazy. They are a myth, a real thing without proof except for those of us who have experienced them. But these are just words. People can take or leave them, mostly leaving them because they want proof—something more than just a story. A long time ago, our ancestors were more open because that is how our history was passed on, by mouth. Nowadays, we are not happy with just words and talking. We have to see things. Why are the same stories spoken a long time ago more important if we read them in a book? I ask myself this in my old age. I fear to ask our young because they will have too many answers. Anyway, my dear one, I am straying."

"Ai-see-ne-suk?" she asks herself. "I don't know. Some say they are good; some say they bring bad things. For myself, they bring company when I am lonely. The days seem longer when you are alone,

Samuel and the Little People

you know. When they come, they talk to me and to each other and are always in good spirits. I feel comfort in hearing them; they are like little kids, especially when they are playing games. I hear their laughter, reminding me of lost memories when I was a child, a time I forgot when I grew up. This makes me happy to feel young again in my old age."

She waved her hand in front of herself. "You see this old, bent body? I cannot run or jump like in my childhood. It is only with memories I can do what I used to do…and those little ones help me recall the past."

She sat there for a long time, lost in her thoughts. I didn't want to break her silence, so we just remained sitting quietly, gazing into the darkness. Quietly, she surprised me with more information.

"They look funny—they are small, like little dolls—and they move so quick. Do you watch the squirrels in the trees? That's what they remind me of."

"What colour are they? Because I've heard others say…" I began, but she interrupted me.

"Colour? I don't know. I never looked at them to see their colour. The ones I talk to, their eyes are dark, not dark as in something bad, but as if they know everything. You get lost in their eyes, but it's not scary. It brings a comfort like when you look at your mom or dad's eyes, and you feel and know they would do anything to protect you. Do you know what mean?" Mrs. J asked.

Mrs. J Talks

I shook my head again.

"Well, you will, soon. They tell me so," she said, the wrinkles in her face scrunching up as she beamed a big smile.

When it was time to leave, I walked away from her cabin as my dad hooked up the horses and began loading up our tools. I stood there, enjoying how different I felt; my mind was lucid, clear, and I was excited to share something so special with someone. I believed her. I really believed her. Looking northeast to our lake, far along the north shore, I could see a dark, foreboding pool in the water. I felt a presence, then jumped when Mrs. J whispered, "Don't ever go there. It is a bad place."

She grinned, knowing what I had been thinking—I was convinced she knew everything I had ever thought.

My father, walking up to us, repeated her warning and placed his hand on my shoulder.

"The Little People say so," Mrs. J said, nodding in a serious manner.

Fire and Deep Water

CHAPTER 3

Fire and Deep Water

I first heard them when I was a child of six and first saw them when I was 12. The Up-See-So Ai-See-Neh-Suk giggled in quick bursts of sound, the same as their jerky squirrel-like movements, as if they feared being discovered. Yet, I found out later they had nothing to fear since they only appeared to humans that they, themselves, selected.

Who of us was lucky enough to be chosen? Or why? Those criteria were from a doctrine long lost or forgotten in the mists of my people's collective memory. Our Elders said the lucky ones favoured to see and hear them were "touched" by a supernatural

Fire and Deep Water

force that deemed they had earned the support the Little Ones offered.

Even if you didn't experience the Up-See-So Ai-See-Neh-Suk as a young person or adult, you still had a chance; the Old Ones said they often came to people in their later years.

Why did they exist at all? Some said they came to protect you, and others said it was to bring a warning of impending doom, while those alone in their old age said they came for comfort and to keep their loneliness away. There were many reasons dreamt up, some unbelievable and some scary, but I saw them as benign and acting in accordance with the way you present yourself to the world and those around you—as a protector, friend, wise person or mystical shaman of warning and prophecy.

It was in the years of the Red Fire that I first heard them as we journeyed from village to village in search of families who had deserted their homes seeking safety from the killing reach of—not an actual fire, but the dreaded disease—smallpox. We came upon a settlement of one-room shacks close to where the pines met the prairie. As we came closer there was a silence bereft of any birds or animals, and even the wind was gone from this place.

My parents called out and received no answer. Far beyond the cabins, tucked under the evergreen trees, were two teepees I could see. I ran to them hoping to find my cousins. My excitement died as fear took hold of my heart, and my legs slowed to a walk. Silence was heavy here, too, as I stopped,

Samuel and the Little People

listened and looked. I stared at nothing for a long while until a shape began to form at the base of some willow bushes behind the lodges.

I took a few more cautious steps, one at a time, as the figure became visible, then another and another. It was the family we were searching for, now quiet and not breathing. I realized this was the death I had heard about. The red spots on them, too many to count, were tongues of flame—the Red Fire—that burned them with pain, fever and scoured the plains as a real fire would.

My mother and father were by me now, each with a hand on my shoulder. They uttered condolences and made a scaffold for the bodies deeper into the pines, offering prayers to the sky. The sun closed the day, so my father made a quick bed of branches to sleep in; he didn't want to unload our tent in this cursed place.

Mother prepared a fire for a small meal while I walked to the scaffold alone. In my innocence, I needed to see them again, and maybe if I went closer to them, I could connect to the love I had for them. I came upon the scaffolds holding the bodies of my uncles, aunts and cousins.

Fire and Deep Water

Under a darkening sky, revealing more stars by the moment, I sat down and stared up to the heavens. I was there with my thoughts, sad to think I would never play with my cousins again, nor hear their voices and laughter. Time disappeared and gradually a calm came over me. Suddenly I was elevated from my dark musings of death; all was peaceful, and I knew from deep within my soul that my family—my relatives—were happy.

A tiny sound interrupted my thoughts; finally, I realized, sound did exist in this sick place. It startled me a little and so I looked to my mother for assurance, but she was quiet, her face aglow in the orange light of the fire she cooked over. There it was again, a chirp, then soft sounds, almost a wailing, but smooth like a song.

I saw movement, shadows flirted with my peripheral vision only to disappear when I looked to see them better. In my ears the noise became tender, harmonious, and I began to understand. We spoke then, that night, as I speak to you.

Finally, my mother called, and I was reluctant to go to her. The Little Ones' talk was so full of meaning that I had to force myself to leave them. As I sat down with my parents, I asked about the voices and the shadows I had seen. They stared at me with fear in their eyes. I saw the distress in their faces, so I quickly reassured them.

"They're not bad."

My father stopped me; his palm held up toward me.

Samuel and the Little People

"Who was there? Be careful of who you talk to!"

"No, they are good people. They talked of my cousins there in kind words, and they told me to beware of bad medicine places and men. They even showed me, Father!" I said, raising my voice.

"How could they show you?" he asked in bewilderment. "And how did they look?"

"I could not see them, only shadows, but they sounded like children...small. And when they spoke, they showed in my head where the bad places were."

My mother glanced knowingly at my father. She said in awe, "Up-See-So Ai-See-Neh-Suk—the Little People!" She looked at me then and put her hands on my head, bringing them down to cradle my face. "You have a gift," she said slowly.

We proceeded on our journey, not knowing where to go but following my direction as I walked according to the vision in my mind. We travelled far and wide, and as we met those we knew were safe in mind and body, our extended family grew to become a village in number. My father would tell of my meeting with the Little People and the vision they had imparted to me. After many days and paths, we settled north and west of where the prairie met the pines.

Thankfully, the Red Fire became no more, and I continued to speak with my Up-See-So Ai-See-Neh-Suk. They were a blessing to me as I always left our meetings in good spirits with their wise and kind words in my ear.

Fire and Deep Water

I was twelve when we decided to move on from our village to a new settlement where some of our family lived. The hunting around our new home was better, and a nearby lake provided fish. It was in the moon of "Returning Geese" when we left, taking 12 days to arrive at our destination.

This band of relations had organized themselves to receive a reservation, and they told us about all the wonderful things the Great White Mother had given them from across the ocean. I didn't see too much of anything while I walked about searching for physical treasures, but then someone explained the treasure given was services received from the government. I didn't see much of this either.

But I did love their land with its lake and abiding hills cascading down to meet the water—tall pine trees fringing its border with pockets of fine sand for beaches. The water was a cool green-blue in the shallow depths and a dark cobalt blue at its deepest end, and it was cold.

The Elders said this part of the lake was so deep that no one had reached the bottom, and many had perished trying. Kids were not allowed in this area—the cold end—where strange things lurked beneath the water and sometimes surfaced to snatch a poor soul, taking him or her down to the lowest depths where no light shone.

We spent long hours in the lake, and it was fine where we swam, but there was always the cold end that beckoned to us. Maybe it was so tempting just because we were not allowed there. People lived away from this area because of the tales of water

Samuel and the Little People

spirits, bad serpents and frog men that waited in the deep. They couldn't breathe out of the water, so people put up their tents and shacks far from the shore, protected from harm's reach. Sometimes a fisherman would come across three-toed tracks in the sand coming from the water, then back into the deep.

One hot day in the moon of "Geese-growing Wings," we walked toward the far end of the lake. Arriving at a spot where we found older men in the lake, crowding the shores with their horses, we sauntered even further toward the deepest water. A few protested, but most of us were filled with a daring bravery, wanting to see what it was that scared older people away.

We sat awhile, gazing at the water and watching for any movement that broke the surface. The water was still, mirror-like, with slow waves that reflected the pines across the lake. The reflections of some small clouds above the trees seemed to dance and sway on the water.

A sudden splash made me jump, and I looked around. Someone had grown impatient, took the dare and dove in. Before long, everyone was in the water yelling and splashing around, not a care in the world. So much for the old wives' tales we had listened to in terror around the fire. We swam, and dove and dunked each other in gleeful abandon for hours until the sun began to set beyond its gold blanket.

"We should go," I said, looking at the horizon.

Fire and Deep Water

"Nooo!" my friends chorused. "Little Samuel is scared."

"I am not!" I shouted in a voice so shrill I hardly recognized it.

"Well, should we stay awhile then?"

"Let's make a fire," someone shouted.

We gathered old beach wood and pines, and soon the flames were reaching the sky, sparks filling the heavens above us with stars. We gazed at the hypnotizing flames, and slowly, as if in a dream, we sat and then laid down, staring up into the blackness of night with tiny, dancing sparks disappearing into it. I was unaware of myself, getting lost in the eternity of space…and time left me.

Something tickled my ear, then I heard a whisper. The voice was disembodied, more of a sudden gust of wind or a puff of air. I jerked awake, and all became clear with the next words I heard.

"Get out! Leave now!" the small voice commanded with urgency. I sat up with a start, eyes wide. I knew the voice from before. It was one of them, the Little People, but as before there was no one, just the voice.

Gathering my thoughts, I took in my surroundings, and my situation came into focus. I had fallen asleep, but now I was all alone. Fear gripped me as I sought and prayed for the person whose words I had heard to appear, to be real. My eyes darted about for this revelation.

Samuel and the Little People

    Something moved in the lake, a ripple, then bubbles rising to the surface…and then…nothing, silence, stillness. The reflection of the full moon was motionless in the water. I sighed with relief.

    In the next moment, something broke the surface, its motion forming a V-shaped wake as it came closer and closer. Both my arms were abruptly encircled by what I thought were branches, but as I looked down, I saw slim, grey fingers. I knew instinctively they belonged to something…or someone…good, and they were helping me to get up. I glanced from one side to the other and, to my surprise, there they were, the Little People. I had no time to marvel at their mystical appearance as I couldn't help but look back to the water and gasp in horror at what was emerging.

    I beheld a dark blue body cutting the surface as a serpent would, its fishy scales glistening in the moonlight and eyes radiating a red glow. I scampered, kicking the air to gain a foothold, but my legs didn't work. I lay there thrashing.

Fire and Deep Water

Before I knew it, the demon was out of the water, standing up on its two hind legs with its short arms extended. It grabbed me, and I felt its claws dig into me as it dragged me out into the deep end.

At my head, two small, greyish beings pulled me by my arms, gradually losing the fight. A shrill cry split the air, but the creature had me past the shoreline and into the water by now. I screamed, knowing my time on this earth was done.

A rash of activity bustled up the shoreline, and noise arose about me. I looked up to see a throng of Little People scrambling into the shallow water, pulling on my arms for all they were worth. Gradually, they overpowered the monster and got me back on land. The creature retreated to its dark lair, disappearing into the cold depths from whence it came. I was laughing, crying and not understanding

Samuel and the Little People

my emotions while I grabbed and hugged each of my saviors.

 Still lying on the sand, I looked closely at them. Nothing about them scared me or made me feel awkward or uncomfortable. They were small; their skin was light green to blue—not grey as I'd first thought—and they had no necks. Their heads were large in comparison to their rotund little bodies, and their arms and legs were as slim as broom handles. They moved as fast and quietly as a squirrel or hummingbird might, and their eyes penetrated mine.

 I looked away, fearing their dark green eyes would see too much of my inner self, but their faces and posture lent me no unrest, confirming as I had always thought—they meant humans no harm. My appreciation of my rescuers was interrupted by the sound of several voices yelling. The sound advanced, and I remembered seeing the older men earlier that day. They must have been responding to my screams.

 The Little People moved quickly, gathering around me in a tight cluster to bid me well and were gone. I blinked once and caught only their motion as they disappeared into the trees and bushes, puffs of dust marking the places where they were absorbed into the ground or the ether.

Fire and Deep Water

The men came rushing from the wagon trail to the grassy side of the shore where I lay, still breathless. Bending over me with concerned expressions, they examined my bloody and bruised leg. Determining these were my only injuries, they sat me up and listened intently as I related my story in a rush of excited words, their eyes darting from the lake and back to me.

They comforted me with low voices, and then two of them examined the strange tracks coming out and back into the lake. One of them, the eldest of the group, limped over to a tree and cut a sheaf of birch bark from its trunk. He measured and then drew the likeness of the monster's footsteps in charcoal on his makeshift paper. I would chance upon his handiwork years later when the old man died, and someone retrieved it from his scant belongings. Remembering the community celebration of me as a warrior who had survived a life-threatening battle, this person handed the sketch to me. At the sight of it, even as an adult, I was transported to that deadly night as though it just happened. I shuddered, and the warm summer air around me turned cold.

I quickly built a small fire and threw it in, watching the edges of the drawing curl up and disappear into flames.

Since that fateful day, my stature among my people grew. I was respected and acknowledged as a gifted person for my ability to see the Little People, and I would see them many times throughout my life and well into my senior years. We would talk, share knowledge and history, or we would make up amazing stories to cheer the children. To this day, I am in their presence. And although I might not see them, nor are they necessarily talking directly to me, their chatter reaches my ears as if they were in the next room. They continue to bring joy and solace into my twilight years.

Napaysis, A Communion

CHAPTER 4

Napaysis, A Communion

    I met him on the trap line when I was only 13. I was young, but I felt like a man when I checked the traps we set, alone and important. If it was really cold, which it often was in those early times, my father or oldest brother would do my job. Furs and hides were our income to buy those precious items we saw at the Hudson Bay stores, and the meat of those trapped animals was our food when deer, elk and moose were scarce.

    Looking back, it was a hard life. But to us it was normal, and we didn't complain. It was all we knew.

Napaysis, A Communion

I'd ventured out about three miles from our family's cabin one day. I was trudging along and sinking to my knees, even with my snowshoes on in the deep, powdery snow. Without the shoes, I'd have lasted maybe half a mile before flopping down exhausted, a very dangerous thing to do when the air was frigid.

Thinking about nothing, I tramped along in the pure whiteness of the new snow, the sun wrapping me in its warm embrace as I absorbed the peacefulness. I was a captive to this wintry world but not a victim. The air and sounds surrounding me were crisp and carried for miles on the still air. My head was down as I followed the old trail, barely visible under the blanket of newly fallen snow. Gradually, I became aware of unusual hills and mounds of disturbed snow here and there…solitary, by themselves. I glanced up, thinking the thing that had kicked up the snow was watching me from the treetops. It had to be because I was alone. But there was nothing there.

Stopping, I bent over in close scrutiny, curious, as to why the little hills were there and what had formed them. Although similar, they were not connected as a trail is, just small poofs and streaks of upturned snow here and

Samuel and the Little People

there. I walked on, noticing by this time that they were quite numerous, dotting the land within my vision.

Overcome by the oddity, I stopped again and chose a hill to dig into. To my surprise, some four feet under the snow, were tunnels! These passageways were approximately a foot and a half in diameter, and they stemmed in all directions.

I thought, *This is weird. I have never seen this before.*

I dug down to the ground, putting my ear to the tunnel opening. I began to distinguish faint sounds that seemed like voices...all similar and familiar. I pushed my head further in to better hear the commotion. I began to think I could hear a soft, rhythmic thumping, movement or footsteps of some sort. Then abruptly, they stopped.

Craning my neck, I burrowed my head further in like a fox. I heard soft noise, a quiet murmur and then more muffled voices...familiar. They became clearer in tone...vibrations to waves, then waves to words. I popped my head above the snow.

"It's them!" I whispered to myself. "Up-See-So Ai-See-Neh-Suk." I had forgotten about them after what happened at the cold end of the water in my childhood.

"The ones who saved me from the Lake Monster," I breathed.

For whatever reason, they had disappeared from my mind, maybe because I didn't want to remember that night. But here I was again, sure that they

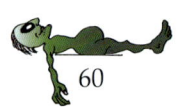

Napaysis, A Communion

were near. I stood up, wondering what to do. I sat and stared down at the hole where the voices were coming from. I decided I should make my presence known then realized that they probably knew I was there and didn't want to be disturbed.

With caution, I called out, my tentative words hanging in the frosty air. "Tansi, hello?" Dead silence met my ears, which had begun ringing.

Then came a response sounding like a voice but with the resonance of a note on a wooden flute. But I knew; I understood.

"Tansi," came the reply from many voices, intoning the word at the same time.

A choir, a harmony with no words, I thought, marvelling at their vocals. I had heard such at school when students spoke or sang in one voice, but that was done on purpose, coordinated, whereas this was spontaneous, done without thought.

From the dark arose a small grey head. I scrambled backward, afraid, but I was still drawn to their vocals, like I read a sailor is drawn to a siren. He, or she, gazed at me; I was unsure of its gender but kept my thought unspoken.

"We have no 'he' or 'she,' but you can call us what you want," it said.

They know. They can read my mind! my inner voice yelled. I checked my panic and steadied myself, realizing the extent of what they knew. I must

Samuel and the Little People

be honest, speak from my heart and be truthful in their presence.

At this thought, it smiled, long thin lips curling at the ends, huge eyes above its nose examining mine. I wasn't uncomfortable now. All seemed right.

In my confidence, I asked, "Do your kind have names?"

"No, we don't. Everyone knows everyone, so there is no need for names. But you can call us what you want; you can give us a name," it replied in harmony.

Names came flooding into my mind from the bible I had read at school: *Adam, Joseph, Peter or even Mary, Martha or Delilah. Delilah?*

What? I can't call him that! I scolded myself, getting flustered again. I calmed down, remembering that gender didn't matter when it came to names. It had said I could call it anything, and so I stilled my mind a moment, gazing at it. It was so tiny, a little man, at least I had thought of it as male right from the start. At that moment, a name popped into my head. Napaysis. It meant "Little Man" in my Cree language.

"So be it, I will call you…"

"Napaysis. Little Man?" it replied in question before I could finish.

"Yes," I said, "You don't like it?"

They all mouthed it in unison, running the syllables over their tongues until it became almost a song.

Napaysis, A Communion

"Yes," Napaysis said. "We will take it. It does have a pleasantness to it."

We talked for hours, and even though it was cold, I felt warm in their prescence. Napaysis spoke of his people at length. I began to learn of their life and asked, if they had no males or females, how was it they had children?

"If we need more, we will join in a circle, meditating about life. If it is to be, and our want is true and just, there will appear in the centre another of our kind. They are born from our thoughts. We are without number across this great world, but few see or hear us. Our thoughts travel through your many lands as we learn about humans near and distant, but there is no need to go and meet others of our family as we know what they know, and they know what we know. We are known by many names by many tribes of your folk: leprechauns, fairies, elves, gnomes, hobbits, Up-sees, but we are all together in mind."

"Why is it that I can see and hear you, yet most of my people cannot?" I asked.

"Because we are the same in mind. Your heart and thinking work in the same tone as ours. Think of singing a song where you cannot separate your voice from ours, or you think the same words as us without knowing. That is being in tone, shining as one."

"And where do you live? I thought it was in the sand and bushes?"

"We live wherever we are by taking the land as it is; we conform to our surroundings. As you now see, we can live anywhere."

Samuel and the Little People

Napaysis' answer brought to mind the isolated hills and longer strips of disturbed snow I had wondered about.

"Why are those mounds of snow there? Are they your doing?"

"Yes. You are a good tracker, Samuel. They happen when we come up for a short breath of fresh air, then go back under to our tunnels. The strips we make when we walk under the snow, having fun or making more tunnels."

"You have fun?" I asked, but my mind focused on the fact Napaysis had just called me by name.

"Why yes, of course we do. Sometimes we even play around with you humans. We have emotions, feelings and moods like you, although not quite the passion and anger you carry. We are a quiet and a peace-loving kind. And yes, we have known you by name for a long time, Samuel." Napaysis smiled.

"Napaysis, can I call you that now?"

"Yes. For you it puts a name to myself."

"Ah yes, true." I reflected on human ways. "Napaysis, I have so many questions. Will I ever see you again to talk and learn more?"

"Oh yes, we will always be near. Now that we shine together, you will never lose us."

Eventually, I arrived back at home. My parents asked why I was so late, worried that I had been injured or taken by the bad spirits of the forest. After I had eaten my mom's stew, I sat for a while, alone, pondering my meeting with Napaysis.

Napaysis, A Communion

Suddenly, a voice chimed in my ear. "Tell them. They will believe." So I did, as everyone sat around the fire crackling in our woodstove.

After the fire died to red coals, I finally stopped, waiting, scared of their reaction. To my relief, my mother and father expressed wonder at my story, but my brother was quiet, considering what I had said. He believed the teachings of our minister that such things were not real, and even if they were, they were "things of the Devil," meant to lead us away from God.

I learned right there and then that night that I should not speak of Napaysis and his kind to just anyone, and if I did tell someone, I should be humble and honest in the stories I was to tell in my life.

Napaysis, or Nap for short, became a close friend. As we shared and made stories, he stayed with me, a muse and brother to the end. I, as a child, read many books loaned to me by our tiny school. But the stories Napaysis told were far from the modern world I was growing up in; they spoke of a simpler and more "connected" time.

Samuel and the Little People

   I never forgot what he told me, and yet it wasn't until I was in mid-life that I took up pen and paper to capture them for others who might appreciate there are things in this world that are still magical and wondrous. I knew there were humans who would love these tales as much as I did.

   We can all "shine."

CHAPTER 5

A Time to Ask

As I grew older, I had fewer responsibilities and more time to ponder upon life. When we are young, we're so busy we don't stop to reflect upon what has happened to us. But now I found my mind filled with questions about past events and time. As a child, I couldn't wait to become an adult and be the boss of my life without my parents telling me what to do. Now, as an old man, I wondered as every aging person must do: why did I disregard time until now, when I found myself desperately wanting back all of the passing minutes and hours I had ignored?

In a melancholy mood, I walked up a hill to sit on its crest. It was a favourite place of mine, perfect for pondering. The late autumn winds had blown

A Time to Ask

the leaves off the trees, leaving golden piles upon the ground. The sky was a deep blue, and I couldn't spot the wisp of a cloud anywhere. Taking off my shoes, I stood on bare ground, my heart beating fast from the climb, exhilarated by the cool air and beauty spread out before me. My mood lifted, and I felt like some kind of god, overlooking my lands.

Napaysis came to mind. He had told me the Little People were timeless, but I wondered what he really meant. Did they question life and time like I did? Did they dwell upon memories from a time almost forgotten? Did they look forward to the future?

The sharp aroma of pine mixed with cranberries enveloped me; I stopped to breathe in the aroma. A soft wind from the west tousled my hair as I breathed deeply to draw in the fragrance. The smell reminded me of my younger days, hunting in the fall with my dad in the bush and helping him stretch fur from animals we trapped. A flood of images exploded in my mind, and in an instant, I was back home as a child sitting on the floor of our log cabin. I felt a warm glow on my cheek as I looked at myself sitting beside an old wood heater.

I was maybe six or seven at that time, gazing around at our simple furniture made by my dad. I saw a beaver pelt stretched over a circle of willow branches, the long guard hairs shimmering orange in the light of the dancing flames. A waft of smoke escaped from the stove, reaching for the ceiling. It encircled the stovepipe, caressing its metal elbow delicately with grey fingers, seeking direction like a blind woman. The smell soothed me, comforted

Samuel and the Little People

me. I was in another world, still thinking about the past and time.

I called to Napaysis.

"Do you know time? How do you measure it? Can you save it as memories?"

My friend was beside me, looking up at me and searching for what my eyes were looking at in the sky.

"A lot of questions, Samuel." Napaysis was knee-high to me as I stood, and he continued to follow my gaze. "You won't find the answer up there in a blank sky. What are you looking at?" he asked with a grin.

"Oh, never mind me. I was daydreaming about my youth. I see visions of when I was a kid, but nobody else can."

"You mean like us, Sam?"

"Well, yeah, that's true, isn't it? Not everybody can see you…if you don't want them to, right?"

"Yes. And we have memories, too, and a past, but we don't measure time as you do. We measure what we have done in our lifetime. Humans are so occupied with time when it matters to them, individually. Whereas we, like plants or animals, live and let it be. Time scares you as you get older, doesn't it Sam?"

His question startled me. He had put into words exactly how I was feeling, but I had avoided admitting my fear of what was coming.

A Time to Ask

"Don't you people die, and don't you wonder about death?" I frowned at him.

"No. When we go, it comes like a quick breeze, a puff of air, then we disappear in a glow, kind of like the light of a firefly blinking out. We don't have sickness, and we don't have events like birth, marriage and death to mark our time here. The natural laws governing us are not the same as yours in your human world. We just go when another comes in, as I told you before."

"I know, but some laws, like time, still govern you, don't they?" I frowned again.

"No, not as you imagine because there is no end to everything after we leave. You believe death is the end of all, but it's just another step."

"Really? What you say brings back the past. Napaysis, let me tell you a story from my youth."

Many, many summers ago, an old wise man came to us on his travels. News of his knowledge and wisdom preceded him, and everyone was hopeful they could sit with him. I was a young man with questions in mind, and I wanted answers to them like everyone else, so I sought him out. I was not allowed to see him 'til all the Elders had smoked the sacred pipe with him. Finally, I was ushered into the lodge where he was sitting. A fire crackled in the middle of the tipi, and someone made sure the medicine man's teacup was kept full. Despite the heat, I shivered in his presence and couldn't keep my voice from trembling.

Samuel and the Little People

"Great Elder, I have but one question."
I waited.

"Speak then, young man." Any confidence I might have had disappeared like water through my hands as his ancient, gruff voice shook my spirit.

"What is time?" I managed to croak.

There was a long pause, and the silence was unnerving. The muffled laughter that broke it made me want to crawl into myself. His reply was a long time coming, as slow as sap trickling from a spruce tree. Still, I waited. Slowly, he raised his hand, demanding quiet. A hush came over the crowd, and while this bear of a man looked about I could hear my heartbeat pounding in my ears.

Expecting him to growl at my question, he instead directed soft words of warning to the others.

"Do not mock his question." He stared at each person sitting in the circle and demanded respect. "Has time clouded your reason that you laugh at he-who-is-without-age? From birth, time will control you and everything in your life; like the night, you will never really know him. He is there, but not welcome." He now had his grizzled hand up, pointing at everyone in the circle, one by one.

"Sometimes you will see him in your children or grandchildren; other times you see him as you gaze upon yourself in still waters. He passes from face to face, so you never forget, but is so common we lose him all the time. Even in the green of spring, the white of winter and the fiery red of the fall, you see

A Time to Ask

him. He is with you all the time and has been since we have had the mind to see him."

Then he posed a question to everyone. "Can any of you explain time and why he is here?"

No one could answer as they thought in silence.

He then turned to me. With comforting words, he gazed into my eyes and managed to make me feel that I, alone, was in his presence and worthy of hearing his answer.

"I am sorry, my son. I do not have the answer you seek, nor does anyone. An ant, the trees or the mighty eagles do not wonder upon this because they live only to live. If all the people were to die, time would remain, but no creature would know him. He is forever in this world. Forever...eternity? This is a measure of time used by us, a name. We need to give place names to that which confounds us, so we think we know it, but we do not know. Time has many names, and like a friend lost in youth, we don't recognize him as we meet. As you get older and wiser, you will get to know him again until, finally, you will not let him leave lest you die. Dying? Don't be afraid. Death is just another world where time is not as we know it in this material world, and dreams live. Time is the reminder of our humanity here on this Earth, but Spirit, the real essence of what we are, knows neither time nor border."

"And that's the end of the story," I said to Napaysis.

Samuel and the Little People

"What your Great Elder told you long ago is the way we think," he commented, deep in thought.

"Yes, now that we've talked, I realize I haven't remembered much of what the old man told me so long ago. And, you know, he had a few final words for me as I stood, and everyone got ready to leave his lodge for their beds. He reached out and put his hand on my shoulder.

I leave these words with you and hope you greet time with a smile when you meet again. Even though you don't think it's possible now, with the straight spine and strong legs you have, some day you will be bent and weak like me. Treat him well; respect him. He is your friend and mentor for life. In your twilight years, when he gives you his hand, take it without fear.

CHAPTER 6

Lost in the City

It felt so good to get back home from where I lived now, the city. Its concrete skyscrapers and black veins of asphalt running through it sapped my soul. I'd rather see rushing rivers and streams than these streets that connect the urban sprawl; they reminded me of Frankenstein's monster, patched together and created by a mad man.

When I got back to the bush, the first thing I did was grab my wood-smoked moccasins from the passenger seat to swap out my hard boots. I slipped on the moose-skin pair my mother had beaded for me—re-soled many times—before I even got out of the car. I walked slowly, feeling the soft earth beneath my feet, a satisfied smile on my face.

Lost in the City

Easily finding the faded paths of my childhood in the pines, I had my old lard tin tucked into my backpack in case I found any berries. I came often, as much as my work and family life would allow. Sometimes I brought my grandchildren to hike the ghosts of trails traversed by man and animal…and the Up-See-So Ai-See-Neh-suk.

I trekked onward down a slope, not really looking but feeling the forest around me, remnants of black-and-white Frankenstein movies still flashing in my mind. My solitude bore down upon me. Old stories I'd heard as a kid about ghosts and bony spectres, like Pakak, haunting the woods surfaced in my mind, and my senses peaked

Sure enough, my worst nightmare was about to come true. I could feel an otherworldly presence. At the far end of the trail, where it disappeared into a curve, stood a dark figure, huge, hunched over and staring at me with its long arms dangling down to its knees.

Sasquatch? Big Foot? I wondered, frozen. The adrenaline that pumped into my heart sent me into a panic, my ears clogging from the pressure of my heartbeat in my ears.

Above the pounding silence, I could detect small echoes of sound below me. I fought to recognize this patter amidst the thundering blare of stillness and terror. When the Sasquatch tilted its head and cried a wail that shook me to my core, a shrill moan crawled up my throat. Things got worse as I felt a tug at my trousers. It wasn't hard enough to pull me down, but it broke

Samuel and the Little People

my pitiful cry. My knees buckled, and I ended up spread-eagled on the ground. Looking down at me was Napaysis, grinning for all he was worth. I looked from his silly face to the beast and then back again. How could he laugh at a time like this?

"Don't scream! You'll scare him!" His incredulous words penetrated the din in my ears and the fog in my brain. For a moment all words escaped me as I stared at the creature and then at Napaysis.

"Scare him? What about me?" My question emerged as a pitiful squeak.

"He's fine; he doesn't bite." Napaysis chuckled in that squirrel-like chatter of his. He laughed, bending over and dropping down beside me to roll around on his fat tummy. "Ahhhh hahaha. You should have seen your eyes!"

I was taken aback by his nonchalant reaction as he stayed on the ground, rolling from side to side.

"That thing is still there, Nap. It could eat us up!" This came out as a desperate shout. My heart had evacuated my throat, but I was still freaked out. "Let's get out of here! Now!" I stood up as quickly as my swimming head allowed.

Lost in the City

"Take it easy," Napaysis said in his harmonious tone. "Look, I will show you." Still on the ground, he squirmed around to face the monster and waved. It stood erect, a good eight feet tall, and raised one impossibly long, hairy arm to wave back!

"Whaaat?" I said, in shock. "I don't believe this!"

"See? Now, you wave. He's harmless…more scared of you!"

"I don't think so, Nap. He doesn't look scared to me; he looks hungry."

"Jeez, all you humans are so judgmental. You think everything is gonna hurt you or eat you. We do not judge. It's not in our nature. Now, wave!"

Timidly, I waved my fingers, not using my whole arm, thinking that waving my arms might scare it, resulting in me being dinner. To my amazement, it waved back, mimicking my wave with its fingers, kind of like Kokum did when the grandkids were leaving, or the queen did when she was in a parade. I smiled at the thought. Sasquatch. Waving to me.

"Wow!" was the only expression I could muster.

"What did I tell you before, Sammy? Just because something is not familiar or is strange to you, doesn't make it bad or harmful."

Napaysis and I started to walk together.

"Was that a Sasquatch?" I asked. "We humans think they are a myth, a legendary beast that kills people."

Samuel and the Little People

"Like us, Sam? Take a look. We are right here before your eyes. Do you think way down inside that we might steal you away or bring bad medicine to you."

"No, no, I didn't mean it that way."

The fact remained, though, my species was paranoid of everything we couldn't put a label on.

"You're right, Napaysis. We scare easily, and we react hastily."

"Those you call Sasquatch have been friends to us Little People for as long as we can recall. We were giants at one time, then grew smaller, but they were always there, our friends. Can you say the same, Sam? Your species have numerous people of different colour and culture but are all human, yet you fight or demean them."

I pondered this and reviewed our history; it was so. Ever since we were "civilized," we thought other tribes and clans were lesser beings.

"I know," I began. "It has been a curse that followed us as we evolved, thinking we were blessed with knowledge and knowing the right way of living. We know little, but think we know it all." I reached down and put my hand on his sloping shoulder. "You are the proof. You know everything yet are humble. You help everybody, yet ask for nothing, you…"

"Stop, Sam," Napaysis interrupted. "You talk too much when you're wrong." He smiled, knowing my thoughts. "Let us sit down, make some Muskeg tea and maybe share a story?"

Lost in the City

"Sure, sure. I'd love that."

Napaysis and I foraged for kindling, breaking some dead branches, and soon had a fire going. I cleaned out my lard pail then drew some water from a pond.

"So where have you been, Nap?" I asked.

"Well, I'm always around. You just have to see me, think hard of me, and I'll come. How about you? We haven't seen you in the forest or on the trapline for a long time."

"Yeah, getting older, Nap. I have a family... even have grandkids now...and still working. So, we moved to the city for education, work and the convenience of buying foods of all sorts."

I suddenly felt guilty about moving away. I had abandoned my old friend and had not summoned him as he had taught me.

"Are you still writing, Sam?"

"Yeah, but not as much as I want...'cause you're not there, Nap."

He erupted in a giggle. "Sam, you don't need me to write."

He knew my excuse was empty. He reached behind him into his little sack and brought out tea leaves and two wee mugs made of pine-sealed birchbark. The water boiled, he steeped the tea and poured it from my lard pail. We sat staring at the fire, sipping.

Samuel and the Little People

Our memories danced in the orange embers, moving, disappearing into the sky, with only the soft crackle disturbing our solitude. Sometimes in sublime silence, words are pointless; it's the presence that matters, where you feel each other. Time had no measure in that spiritual enclave of pines.

Soon, memories dropped slowly, like ash from the dying embers wafting into our consciousness. In synch, we mumbled some names of friends, most of them gone now. We had broken our silence. We spoke, shared stories about old friends from the days of my younger years to the present, and how time had changed things so much, yet certain malignant values learned from ignorance and hate persisted to the present.

We sat in that clearing for a long while, the towering pines above us swaying gently in the breeze. It was idyllic, and then the soulful sound emanating from the creaking trees sent a slight chill crawling up my spine. We looked up at each other, one name from the past entering our minds at the same time.

"Richard," I whispered.

"Two-Hearts," he responded, surprising me. Were we both thinking of the same person?

Richard Two-Hearts was an old friend to both of us from sixty years before, although I was not aware that Richard knew of the Little People until I was in my twenties. He was a strong man in character, life and values and staunchly believed in his fellow man. He came from the old family

Lost in the City

and tribal beliefs, customs that honored men of such standing and was known only as Two-Hearts until the missionaries dictated that he must have a first name, henceforth Richard.

"You knew him too, Nap?" I asked.

"Oh yes, for the longest time, and such a nice fellow. I miss him."

"I knew he died, but how did he meet his Creator?"

"To tell the story where it ends, we must know how he got there. So I will briefly recall his past, then you can finish."

I took the pen and pad from my backpack that I always had to jot down ideas and do sketches.

Two-Hearts was born into a history most would rather forget. The Treaties had been signed, so across the nation, Indians were imprisoned on government reservations. Some may argue that I can't use the term "imprison," but no other word can describe the situation. Your people could not go out anyplace or anywhere from the reserve without written permission.

Napaysis paused. "Sam, you must tell about the laws that bound Richard to the rez, then to their schools."

"Uh huh," I muttered. "I know them well. I will write notes as I go…for a story," I added, returning to my notepad.

Samuel and the Little People

When Two-Hearts was five years old, he was abducted and taken to the residential school where he was to be civilized and become a Christian. None of the Indian ways were to be tolerated, so he and all the others suffered physical abuse for any display of their culture by way of the strap, beatings or isolation and starving. There were many, many children wrenched from the arms of their parents. They were gone for months until school was out. Some stayed there all of their school years, never going home because some had lost their parents to alcohol or death as a result of them being taken in their school years. For them, there was no home to return to. So, they made their way to the city.

Richard was one of those. He never went home or saw his parents alive. He attended their funerals, both in one year, and nobody knew him as he stood by their graves in his dark suit. I suspect this was about the time he started to drink and seclude himself. He shunned contact with anybody from the reserve, including his relatives. He had been brainwashed into becoming a Christian and made to feel shameful of the old ways of his people. Then, suddenly he found himself, and he turned again to his culture.

"This was about the time you met him," I interjected. "Right, Napaysis?"

I lifted my pen, waiting for his response.

Yes. Before we met, he had doubts, anger and no identity. He was lost in this new world and

Lost in the City

outside of his culture, but he listened. One evening, taking swigs from a bottle of rye whisky, he went for a walk, ending up in the willows along the river where he passed out. Upon awakening, feeling decrepit and sick, old memories came to him, and he called to his parents in a cry. That was when we visited him, by the river, at one of the saddest moments of his life. We talked to him for a long time and did our best to build him back up. Soon, he was reaching out to Elders and people of knowledge for the ways he had lost. He took in all the good things of his culture, and with a kind heart he practiced what he learned, making sure the old people had enough firewood and flour, and tending to their every need. We had many talks, and he told us he was happy, proud of who he was.

I added my recollection to our story.

    Yes, after a few years back on the reserve, he met a woman, Eva, very pretty, and they got married. They had a boy and a girl. The boy, born first, was named Abraham; the girl's name was Mary. As the kids grew, he established himself in the community by helping anyone and everyone. He became well respected. He received many thanks; he was indeed happy. It should have been a fairytale life and ending, but the residential schools were now in their prime, their power backed by Federal Government laws. They exercised their thoughtless authority cruelly over all of Canada. Unwarranted, and with no notice, they swept into our communities and claimed all children

Samuel and the Little People

five to seventeen, carting them off in cattle trucks to the schools far away.

They came to Richard's reserve, and he was there when they arrived with the RCMP and Indian Agents, who controlled the reserve. Richard was apprehensive, knowing the abuse he and many others had survived, but the agent and a priest persuaded Richard to let them take Abraham. They warned Richard that he could be thrown in jail if he resisted, leaving the rest of his family alone, destitute and starving. They lied through their teeth, telling him the schools were so different, better now than in his day. So, he relented with a heavy heart.

I paused and stirred the embers in the fire pit.

"Nap? This is painful to remember."

"I know," he said, eyes fixed on the ashes. "You have to finish, though. You have to write, so people know."

The first promise was broken when Abraham didn't come home for Christmas as agreed to by the authorities. Richard wrote the priest but got no reply. He wrote again. Nothing. It was getting close to Easter when he got permission to leave the reserve to go to town for groceries. There, he found a phone, and with the help of a kind, elderly lady, he managed to find where his son was being schooled. Immediately, he returned home with a sense of dread, explaining to his wife that

Lost in the City

he must go. He quickly bundled up a couple of blankets, tea and bannock while Eva got the horse ready. He was off on his journey that would be four days long, provided the old mare the kids had named Ben could carry him without stopping too much.

I hesitated, straightening my back. Nap was staring into the fire, the night reflected in his big, dark eyes. I reached for my miniature cup, dipping it into the tea, then dipped it again and again. Four of these cups were equal to one human cup. The red lard pail sat precariously on the glowing coals, tilted at a dangerous angle. With my pine branch poker, I lifted the tea pail, then set it down squarely. I did not want to enter this part of Richard's story.

I looked at Napaysis, sitting comfortably on his cushion of moss, as natural to the forest as the plants and trees.

"Hey, Nap. What are you thinking?" I asked, buying more time.

"Hmm," he breathed, rubbing his chin and thinking hard. "Why are your many tribes of people across the world so hurtful to each other?"

"I think we are made that way, then we have to unlearn through care and thought as we grow older."

Nap was silent.

"Anyway, I should go on. My fingers are getting stiff from the cold since the fire went out.

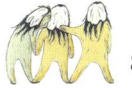

Samuel and the Little People

Guess I'm getting old, eh Nap?" I chortled at my pitiful attempt at a joke; he sat like a rock.

Four mornings passed as Two-Hearts continued to the school. By mid-day of the last, he came across a road, one made by those giant tractors. He rode in the bank of the ditch, for maybe an hour, then up on a hill, he could finally see an enormous building of stone. Richard scouted the area, making sure there were no RCMP about. It was clear, so he rode up the cement pathway to the entrance; cringing at the clopping sound his horse made. Soon, a few kids noticed him, and then a priest came out. The priest's black robes swayed in a defiant manner as he strode aggressively toward Richard, who was immediately transported back to his childhood. He remembered seeing anger in authority figures, and it spelled trouble.

Nothing has changed, he thought. *This man is violent, and his actions speak louder than words.*

The priest grabbed the reins, hollering in anger.

"What are you doing here? No adults can be here!"

With his horse reeling backward, Richard dismounted and snatched back the reins.

"I have come for my boy," he said in an angry, but subdued voice. His mind opened as a flood of memories pulled him down into a whirlpool of abuse and helplessness. Not one had anything pleasant in it. His anger was mounting. The priest recognized this and took a step backward.

By this time, another priest, much older, came out from the school to ask what was going on. Richard, in halting English, described the letters he had written about his son and how his worry was magnified when there were no replies. The older priest asked both men to follow him to his office upstairs, a dark mahogany room with sculpted cherubs of plaster in each corner that listened with false smiles as the three men sat down at a huge oak desk. The priest spoke slowly, as though he thought Richard would not understand what he was about to say. It was a school rule that no visitors could come to the school unless called for by him or an appointment was made. Richard explained that no one had followed these rules when they came and got him as a child, and later took his son.

"Well, the Indian agent approved us taking both you and your son. Notices were sent out to you through him."

Richard knew he was lying. His distrust of the white newcomers made him feel sick, and he knew he should never have given his permission for them to take Abraham.

Why did I let him go? he asked himself. *I should have hidden him.*

With this thought, he stood and bluntly demanded to see his son. The priests were persistent about the "no visitor" rule, but Richard was unrelenting, threatening to bring a horde of parents from his community to demand the release of their

Samuel and the Little People

children. This seemed to cause the black robes some concern, so they agreed, this once, that they would let him see his own son, providing there was no further trouble, or else the boy would be denied the right to go home for Easter. Richard knew these consequences were true, since other parents he knew had suffered the same punishment. Richard nodded in agreement.

I paused and took a breath. "Napaysis?"

"Yesssss…?" he answered, dragging out the "s."

"Do you think people outside will believe this? I'm taking notes to remember later, to keep each memory separate, but I see, in fact, I know, that there are many other stories like this that were told to me, yet nothing has ever been done about it. No government, priest, bishop or RCMP has stopped and listened to us."

"That is why you can't stop writing this down. This is a different time, Sam, and maybe it's the right time."

"I know, but the remembering is hard, especially when nobody listens."

"Uh huh," he whispered.

I saw that he was still staring at the pail holding our tea. I knew what he was thinking; other kids used old lard pails to take their lunches to day school, and they managed to escape or hide from the raids to collect residential

Lost in the City

school students. These day schools were built by Indigenous leaders with the government as a partner and were stationed on each reserve that had signed for such schools, and, supposedly, the parents had more say in the schools. But still, some were just as bad, ruled by dictator teachers, preachers or priests. At least the kids could go home after school each day.

Napaysis poked the fire and straightened the pail again. Hundreds of embers flew up into the sky.

"Okay then, let's finish. The sun will be coming up soon," I joked.

Mulling over what words to begin with, I jotted down a few before I started talking. Napaysis was still silent, so I prompted him. "Okay. So, as they are sitting in that room, that majestic, dark and kind of foreboding place, that seems to represent 'right and wrong' with those idyllic, baby angels looking down, the older priest asked Richard for the name of his son.

"Abraham. Abraham Two-Hearts," Richard answered immediately.

The old man stared at him for bit. Then, in the silence, the two priests looked at each other, and Richard sensed something was wrong. But the sounds of children shouting outside the open window filled his ears, and he decided it must be recess. He brushed his fear away and thought, *Maybe Abraham is out there.*

Samuel and the Little People

"What's his name again?" the older priest asked, lowering his voice. He looked down and a furrow appeared in his brow. "And...how old is he?"

"Abraham Two-Hearts," Richard repeated. His growing apprehension made him impatient with the question being asked again. "He is six years old," he almost shouted.

The two priests looked at each other, and once more, the gloomy silence seemed to last forever. Richard squirmed in his chair of mahogany wood, dark wine in colour and hard as rock.

Why are they getting so uneasy? he wondered.

"Father David," the old priest said. "Please bring me that book."

He directed the younger priest to an ominous-looking black book on a shelf. The younger priest placed it in front of his superior with a thud, and the old one leafed through several pages, running his boney finger down each one.

"We don't have an Abraham Two-Hearts here, do we?" he said finally, asking the question in an unsteady, quiet voice. The younger priest leaned in toward him and shook his head "no."

Richard jumped up and grabbed the book. "You're lying!" he shouted, turning the pages one at a time, finally sitting to rest the book on his lap because it was so heavy.

He continued thumbing through it carefully. *So many pages,* he thought to himself.

Lost in the City

He continued on, getting to the "R" section and saw the name Abraham, with the last name Roberts. He showed the name in the book to the old priest.

"What is this?" he asked, pointing to a crossed-out name he barely made out as Two-Hearts.

"Oh, we changed his name to "Roberts," the old priest replied. "Because his name was too confusing."

Richard threw the book down, not having read the writing under his son's first name. The book landed in an explosion of dust particles, dancing in the rays of light coming from the window. Then, as the dust settled, he noticed the book had landed open to the first page. He read the word "DECEASED," written in capital letters across the top. Momentarily, Richard's mind could not comprehend the meaning of the word. He sat down, staring at the black book, knowing without reading it that his son's name was on this page, written in spidery script.

The two black figures bobbed toward him.

As death would move, Richard thought.

He felt hands on his shoulders and a faraway voice telling him his son had contracted pneumonia and died before Christmas. He was buried immediately. At last, through tears, Richard asked where his son was.

"Behind the school."

"Take me to him!" Richard demanded, brushing their arms away as he walked toward the door, tears

Samuel and the Little People

streaming down his face. Somehow, with blurred vision, he found an exit door at the end of a long hallway. Standing on the steps, his eyes scanned the breadth of the backyard, and he noticed there were no tombstones, just wild, scraggly grass and a fence that looked like broken teeth, its paint long gone. He hurried out to the sad patch of ground that stood for the school cemetery, searching for any indication of his son's resting place. He looked pitiful, turning slowly in a circle, his shoulders sagging.

A group of boys had been watching Richard, sensing something was wrong, out of place in this otherwise ordinary day. The man was as dark-skinned as they were, familiar, like the uncles and older cousins from back home they seldom saw anymore.

"What is he doing in the graveyard?" the oldest of them wondered. No one went near the gloomy place if they could help it.

The oldest boy was a tough kid—he had to be in this horrible place—but something tugged at his

Lost in the City

heart, and he approached the man. His two sidekicks followed.

"Sir, have you lost someone?" he asked in a hushed tone. "Do you speak Cree?"

The other two boys backed away a bit, knowing their mouths would be washed out with soap, and they would get no supper if the priests heard anyone speaking their mother tongue.

Richard didn't bother to look. He mumbled his son's name. The boys spoke in Cree, and Richard heard them say, "Abraham Two-Hearts."

The oldest boy pushed his younger friend forward.

"A-Abraham was my best friend, but he's gone now." The rail-thin boy dug his doubled-up fist into his eyes, trying to squeeze back the tears. The breeze blew the grass, and an awkward silence descended.

Finally, the older boy spoke. "They beat him up. Then he died."

Richard turned to the group, a forbidding look on his face. The boys stepped back, scared he would strike them like the priests did when they said something the black robes didn't like.

"Where is he?"

"We don't know. There are so many here. We see kids one day, then we don't see them the next. I saw the priests, from the dorm window, burying something in here at night once. But I don't get up at night anymore."

Samuel and the Little People

One of the boys pointed to a thicket east of the fence and west to some lilac trees, showing Richard how big the cemetery was. Richard scoured the yard and bush but found nothing. His sorrow turned to rage as he strode back into the school, vowing to kill the old priest. But the alarm had been sounded, and a wall of clergy wrestled him to the ground. They managed to tie his arms behind his back and escort him off the grounds.

The RCMP officer who had been called stood by Richard's horse and watched him mount. He warned Richard that he would throw him in jail if he came back to bother the priests.

Richard pretended to leave but only hid his horse and himself in some willows beside a nearby stream until the sun went down. By the light of an almost-full moon, he rode back and crept into the graveyard, tying a length of cotton cloth he kept in his pack around a poplar tree in the thicket. It was a spiritual custom to honour those who had passed on, but Richard never imagined he would be marking the death of his own son with it.

Later, he tried to break into the school, but iron bars covered the doors and windows, like a prison. He made his way home and found it wasn't the same place anymore. Abraham was his oldest son, his favourite child. He was crushed, inconsolable and beyond even the soothing words of his wife. Then he started to drink and drank himself into a stupor. He blamed himself for Abraham's death. The authorities had talked him into letting his son go, and Richard had betrayed him. He thought of the priests

Lost in the City

beating his boy to death. He could not yet allow his mind to visualize what happened.

"That is such a sad story, Nap," I said, putting down my pen and pad, wiping a tear away quickly. Napaysis noticed my action.

"Why hide your emotions? Cry. All should cry for the torture your people's children endured."

"I have cried, but my tears have run dry. It has been a long time of remembering and none outside share our grief because they don't know. Today's schools don't have it in their history."

"That is why your people should write; more should come out, not just to record the bad but the good, too. We are kindred to you and the earth, and there is much joy and humour to tell."

"I agree, Nap." I take up my pen. "Let's finish.

Samuel and the Little People

After Richard returned and failed to deal with his sorrow, I lost contact. He did leave his wife Eva and daughter Mary—not a good thing—but he did it. Too much pain and despair to give anything positive to his family."

"Where did he go, Nap?"

We had also been out of touch. In his grief, Richard never called out for help. He became a vagabond, a dishevelled bum in the back alleys of towns, then he went to the city, Saskatoon. He was loathe to have any company except whatever bottle of alcohol he could find. He sat on a corner during the day begging for money, and at night, he drank himself to sleep. We came across him one night while we were picking herbs along the riverbank. He remembered us, so we spoke there in a small clearing in the twisted willows. Despite all his suffering, depression and addiction, he was still a soft-spoken fellow who had no anger left in him; he was just beaten down. We tried to reach him, to help him return to his home or to find his spiritual connection to the Earth, but all ties had withered. There were a few friends, and even some of your social workers tried to help him. The rest avoided him, scared because of his appearance. The years of grief and hard living had ravaged him. He looked like that Sasquatch you feared. No one wanted to go near him.

I recalled the tall, hairy beast as I scribbled, feeling foolish over my earlier fright.

Lost in the City

"Images are so strong, Sam. Richard saw no reason to change."

He was numb to life so he wandered the back alleys, suppressing any images that haunted his mind, but he could not escape the odd flash of memory. The reality of those memories was a nightmare from which he could not escape, even in slumber. He saw his loving wife and his beautiful daughter, but the image he cowered from and that overpowered everything—the one he had tried to shut out—was the beating of his son, crying out with no one to help. Then he was gone, taken by a bottle to another world, to another nightmare. This went on and on. We would visit, but the truth is we couldn't help him if he didn't want it.

But I couldn't forget Richard. One night, I braved the city by myself, venturing into the dark alleys. It was easier with one because two or three of us couldn't hide in the shadows. It was pretty cold that night, and it had snowed. The streets were ice, and I worried that Richard would freeze if he was sleeping outside. I found him huddled beside a metal door, wrapped in an old, quilted blanket. The blanket was old, patches tethered by weathered yarn, and it didn't offer much protection.

"Hello Richard," I whispered in a low voice. He turned to me, lifting his head from the blanket. He said, "Hi." And then he asked, "Why do you keep coming to find me?"

"Because we are kin, Richard," I reminded him. "Because we are of the same Earth."

Samuel and the Little People

I talked for an hour, imploring him to follow me home to the willows and then maybe to his home. He thanked me but said no; he was waiting for Abraham—his Abe—and he talked like his son was still alive. I couldn't do anything but leave him there.

But when I got back to my people, everyone knew about Richard and how he was slipping away. We risked harm and went as a group to try to carry him to safety. We decided to bring him to live with us and hoped he would return home when he felt better.

Oh, we were sneaky that night, slipping from shadow to shadow, hiding behind trash cans, sliding along cars, not wanting to be seen and possibly harmed by humans. But when we got to him, he had frost on his hair and eyebrows, and one bare arm was outstretched, blue with cold. He was almost gone. We gathered around him like buffalo do when one of their herd is down; each of us touched him. Then, his hand moved, and he beckoned us closer. We crowded in to hear his faint words.

"I see Abe," he said, and his last breath escaped in a cloud. He was no more.

I looked at Napaysis and repeated Richard's last words.

The little man rubbed his eyes and silently put out the remaining coals with the leftover tea and grounds. They hissed and disappeared to vapour, the steam reaching into the sky. My eyes followed the wispy ghosts of the dying fire as they reached

Lost in the City

for the stars, and I knew Richard and Abraham were happy now…no troubles.

It had been hard to get through the story, but I found a sense of peace in hearing Napaysis talk about Richard's last moments. He had some good in his life before his son was taken from him. He could not be faulted for the feelings of loss and guilt consuming him. The newcomers had taken a loved one and even his culture away from him.

What people walked around and avoided that morning in the back alley was a very good person, not the dishevelled and dirty homeless Indian they disdained and feared.

I looked down the trail and glimpsed the Sasquatch still standing there. He waved goodbye to me, and I waved back, a grin on my face. I had changed my thinking about him.

"Such sad stories, so many you could fill an entire book, eh?" Napaysis remarked.

"You think so. Should I?" I watched his face, blue with small wrinkles. He turned his huge, dark eyes to me, brushing his long, obsidian hair over his shoulders.

"Do it. Maybe someone will listen. Some kid out east will learn something. Maybe even an adult or two."

"I will, Nap, I will."

We parted that night, but not for long. After I promised to finish the book, he became my muse, writing coach and lifelong friend.

Samuel and the Little People

"And, Samuel, open your eyes. Look deeper into things and don't be so scared when you do," Napaysis called, as he walked deeper into the trees along the paths of my childhood, and I emerged from them on my way back to the city. His thin voice carried easily in the darkness, and I smiled to myself. He always had to have the last words, and they were always profound.

I looked up to see a cloud in the otherwise clear sky. I could envision a loving father—a wonderful man—and his adoring son, wrapped in a blanket together, going to the sun as it set.

The Old Storyteller

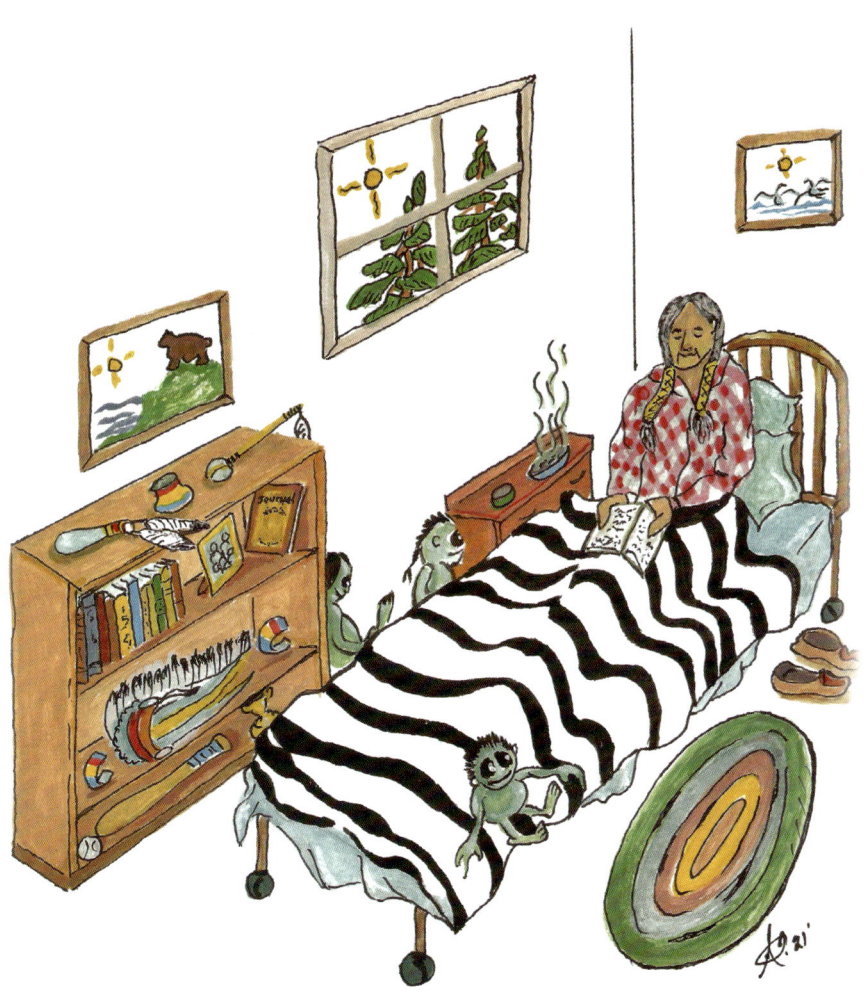

CHAPTER 7

The Old Storyteller

In the evening light, the cracks in the rawhide rattle looked like spiderwebs someone had darkened with India ink, and the feathers of the eagle wing fan were obscured by dust settled over many years. Along with his other treasures, the shelf-top collection looked like a still life—an ode to a spiritual warrior—waiting to be cleaned and placed under museum glass for all to see.

His quilt was a treasured blanket sewn in black and white to signify spirit and reality, loyalty and victory, his colours anointed at adolescence. It kept him warm, underneath the

The Old Storyteller

cherished buffalo robe he had been given many years ago, one he could never part with. His fingers caressed the blankets with the soft touch he had used to smooth the foreheads of each of his newly born grandchildren when they cried. Tonight, he visualized each one as they stared in wonderment at the new world around them. Yet, some had refused to open their eyes, maybe wanting to go back into the safe, warm world they had just left, scared to begin their new life.

And what lay ahead for him, he who was at the end of his? Looking out the window he imagined what form his Paradise would take, if there was one. He saw the eagle fan and rattle he had used when he told stories to his children, grandchildren and their friends, thousands of listeners probably. His props were nearing their end, too. The red paint on the rattle was cracked, and the feathers of his fan were frayed.

Laying his head back on the pillow, he stared at the log cabin ceiling, exhausted as his memories flashed before him. Good memories, mostly, and some he would rather forget—those of friends, family and even children who had died before their time. But then, he should accept these, too, because soon he would greet them again. It was what he was leaving behind that saddened him—the faces of his great grandkids smiling and laughing. His eyes watered, and tears followed the paths of his wrinkles to drop off his chin.

Small voices reached his ears. He thought his grandchildren were back but glanced around to see he was alone. The sounds became louder,

Samuel and the Little People

mingled with the bright laughter he found familiar. The chatter emitted from the dark corners of his cabin, flitting from one side of the room to the other.

"Are the kids playing tricks on me?" he wondered aloud, but then smiled at his question as he realized his grandchildren were too big to hide and didn't play such games anymore.

His room became quiet, and he propped his body on his elbows as his eyes searched every nook and cranny. Nothing. He fell back on his pillow, wondering if he was losing it. The thought scared him as he envisioned a withered, ranting old man no one wanted to be near. He checked out the window.

"Yes, the real world is still there," he assured himself.

He looked down at the veins crossing his hands and looked out of his peripheral vision, glancing sidelong at his surroundings in the way you look for ghosts or spirits. Not focusing, he saw common objects around him. There was the rocker, its arms rubbed smooth with use, the dresser tilted with drawers not quite fitting in their slots and the lamp with its dull, grim light.

He looked away, disgusted at this keen awareness. Time was all around him and insistent that he recognize it, a heavy cloud snubbing the sun. He had been bedridden for a long while, and the situation wore at his will. Pain

The Old Storyteller

was a constant companion. He knew his life had been good, especially compared to others he had known, but the living right now was harder than dying.

A movement caught his eye. Squinting, he peered into the dark corner as a figure with a childlike body emerged. The short, quick steps it took to reach him awoke a forgotten memory. It all came back to him as he recalled the Up-See-So Ai-See-Neh-suk who had graced him with visits and stories of a time forgotten.

Not everyone could see them, and the Little People only showed themselves to those they saw as honoured friends who had done things for them. In his case, they favoured him for the stories he told and wrote in his later life as he learned the white man's way of writing. This tiny person, to whom he had given the name Napaysis, "Little Man" in his Cree language, had become a close and dear friend. The old Storyteller, in his old age, had lost contact with his friend.

"Is that you, Napaysis?"

"Yes," the tiny figure said in a voice matching his size. "How are you doing, old friend?"

"Not well," the Storyteller responded. Then he brightened and asked where Napaysis had been throughout the years.

"Why did you not visit all this time? You told me stories for many years and then you were gone. I missed you. I missed our talks."

Samuel and the Little People

"Samuel, I was always here. You just couldn't find me in all your shadows." Napaysis' smile warmed the Storyteller, and an understanding passed as their eyes met.

"We have one more story to write," Napaysis said.

Samuel understood his meaning and grinned. "Yes we do. I've been ready. Ready for a while."

Napaysis jumped to the edge of the bed and nestled into a worn pillow.

"How should we start? You want this short, right Sam?"

"Yes. Simple, yet thoughtful. And everlasting."

"You don't ask for much, do you?" Napaysis chuckled, and Samuel nodded in agreement.

He looked at the old man expectantly, but a cloud passed over the Storyteller's face. He stared out the grimy window.

"Okay, I'll help," Napaysis said. "Listen, and then write after me."

He looked at Samuel and wove his long white hair through his fingers. Slowly, he drawled, "In a time not that long ago, and on land not that far away, was an old Storyteller…"

He stopped and waited.

The old man repeated the words, then faltered. He stared at his gnarled hands, hoping they might rekindle his memory, but they lay

The Old Storyteller

there in the folds of the quilt made in a time long past. He wriggled his fingers, but they couldn't pluck memories from thin air.

"I have a story for you," Napaysis said, seeing his dear friend in despair. "One last story." He straightened and touched the old man's cheek tenderly. Samuel waited for the words, stoic.

Silence descended upon the room until the old man spoke.

"I am waiting for the words, Napaysis."

"You know the story, Samuel."

"Sorry, my friend, I do not know what you speak of. I am out of stories."

The dark, deep pools of Napaysis' eyes shone in the lamplight. A few other Little People had climbed onto the bed and snuggled under the shaggy old buffalo robe. Napaysis began.

"A long time ago…I was born to the one called Stands Strong Woman and her man Many Buffalo in a camp by the Sasakimo River. I was named Storyteller by my Kokum, who saw me in a dream telling many stories."

The old man sat up abruptly. "Wait! That's my story!"

"Yes, it is, my old friend." Napaysis stood up on spindly legs and waved his arms to indicate the relics around the room. "Look about you, Sam. You have so many

Samuel and the Little People

memories in this cabin, right here. Now you write. This is your story."

The old man found a new energy and rose from his bed. On a table made by his Moshum from the wood of an old wagon, he sat each day for as long as his ancient bones would allow. As he spoke and shared stories about his life with Napaysis, a pile of pages grew, holding stories of not only the old man but also those of people who had helped him grow. His hand ached, and his back protested, but he patted the paper that held his scribbles with love, just as he would his great granddaughter's head.

When he was finished, he looked at Napaysis and his gaze said, "Now what?"

"Just take my hand. We are going to dream and climb aboard a handsome birchbark canoe, finely stitched with spruce root by the nimble fingers of my people."

The old man fell asleep, and Napaysis stayed beside him until, a little later, the cabin door creaked open. In the light of a full moon, a beautiful woman with a kerchief around her head entered, followed by her lovely, black-haired daughter.

The mother looked lovingly at her sleeping grandfather then busied herself starting a fire to boil water in a dented kettle upon the iron stove.

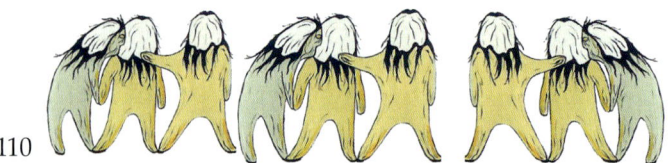

The Old Storyteller

"We should have come sooner, but that moose meat took so long to dry," she worried out loud as the flames began to crackle. The girl sat by the sagging bed, searching under the quilts for her great grandfather's hand so she could entwine her fingers with his.

Strange, she thought to herself. *Why won't he wake up?*

"Mom?"

"Yes…?"

"I think Moshum is gone."

Arnold James Isbister

Arnold is a band member of the Ahtahkakoop Cree Nation in Saskatchewan, Canada. He recalls growing up without modern amenities under the infamous "pass system" that required his parents to obtain permission from the band's Indian Agent to leave the reservation for any purpose, even to sell grain, cream or eggs for income. With no roads, electricity or television, he occupied his time listening to the Elders tell stories and illustrating them. Many are captured in his other books *Stories Moshum and Kokum Told Me* and *Strange Bannock*. *Stirbugs and Screws* is derived from his work at a psychiatric centre for the criminally insane. You can find his writing in anthologies, magazines (*Transition*, Sask Archives) and a CBC radio Legacy Project entitled *Folklore, Myth and Legends*.

Arnold loves the outdoors and walking in the woods. He continues to write and is an award-winning author and artist whose work resides in the collection of HRH Prince Charles. He taught visual arts to at-risk youth and continues to mentor emerging artists. He recently completed permanent illustrations for the World Heritage Wanuskewin Park and Mewasin Trail in Saskatoon, Saskatchewan.

You can contact Arnold at: arnoldisbister@hotmail.com

Meeting His Royal Highness Prince Charles